LIFE SCIENCE

PLANTS

Jonathan Bocknek

WEIGL PUBLISHERS INC.

Project Coordinator
Heather C. Hudak

Design
Bryan Pezzi

Cover Design
Terry Paulhus

Published by Weigl Publishers Inc.
350 5th Avenue, Suite 3304, PMB 6G
New York, NY 10118-0069

Website: www.weigl.com

All of the Internet URLs given in the book were valid at the time of
publication. However, due to the dynamic nature of the Internet, some
addresses may have changed, or sites may have ceased to exist since
publication. While the author and publisher regret any inconvenience
this may cause readers, no responsibility for any such changes can be
accepted by either the author or the publisher.

Library of Congress Cataloging-in-Publication Data

Bocknek, Jonathan.
  Plants / Jonathan Bocknek.
    p. cm. -- (Life science)
  Includes index.
  ISBN 978-1-59036-717-9 (hard cover : alk. paper) -- ISBN 978-1-
59036-718-6 (soft cover : alk. paper)
  1. Plants--Juvenile literature. I. Title.
  QK49.B556 2008
  580--dc22
                              2007012637

Printed in the United States of America
1 2 3 4 5 6 7 8 9 0 11 10 09 08 07

Every reasonable effort has been made to trace ownership and to
obtain permission to reprint copyright material. The publishers would
be pleased to have any errors or omissions brought to their attention
so that they may be corrected in subsequent printings.

Contents

What Do You Know about Plants?

Did you know that this book is made from plants? Plants are used to make paper. Are you sitting in your favorite chair or reading in bed? Plants are also used to make the furniture in your house.

■ Plants come in all shapes and sizes, from a small cactus to a towering tree.

Parts of your house are made from plants, too. When you are hungry, plants nourish you. When you are ill, certain medicines made from plants can help you feel better. Plants even make the **oxygen** in the air you breathe. Plants make Earth a living planet. More than 250,000 different kinds of plants live on Earth. They are divided into two main groups.

Flowering Plants
This group includes plants that produce flowers. Most of the plants on Earth are flowering plants.

Non-flowering Plants
The second group includes plants that do not produce flowers. These are referred to as non-flowering plants.

Puzzler

What are the first living things astronauts can see when they are flying back to Earth from space?

Answer: Plants. As their spacecraft gets closer to Earth, astronauts can see the green leaves of tall forest trees.

Plants Make Food for Everyone

Animals have to eat to get food. Plants make food for themselves.

Plants need three things to make food—sunlight, water, and **carbon dioxide**. Inside their leaves, plants have a green-colored substance called **chlorophyll**.

■ **Plants use sunlight and water to make food.**

Chlorophyll lets plants use sunlight to change water and carbon dioxide into sugar. Sugar is the food plants make to nourish themselves.

Plants use food to grow and stay healthy. Animals use food for the same reason. All animals, in one way or another, depend on plants for food.

Activity

Name the "Eaters"

1. Name two animals that eat plants. What plants do they eat?

2. Draw a picture of yourself and the foods you like to eat. Are you a plant-eater? Are you an animal-eater? Are you both?

■ Some animals eat only plants for food. They are called herbivores, which means "plant-eaters."

7

Plant Parts

M ost plants have three main parts—roots, stems, and leaves. Roots keep a plant anchored in the ground. They collect water and minerals from the soil.

■ **Trees and grass have roots that stretch out in all directions.**

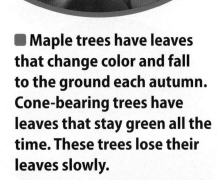

Stems hold a plant's leaves up to sunlight. They also move water, food, and minerals to different places inside the plant.

Leaves contain chlorophyll, which helps leaves make food for the plant.

 Maple trees have leaves that change color and fall to the ground each autumn. Cone-bearing trees have leaves that stay green all the time. These trees lose their leaves slowly.

Puzzler

Each autumn, the leaves of many plants change color before they drop to the ground. Do you know why this happens?

Answer: Leaves contain chemicals that are different colors. As the days get shorter and the nights get colder, the green chlorophyll goes out of the leaves. Other colored chemicals, such as red, yellow, and orange, then become visible. The colors are there during the spring and summer, but the green chlorophyll covers them up until autumn.

9

Life Cycles

L ike all living things, plants have a beginning, then they grow, **reproduce**, and die. This series of changes that a living thing goes through is called a life cycle.

A maple tree starts from a seed in the ground. Roots push down, and a stem pushes up. When leaves form, the young tree can make its own food. When it matures, the tree produces seeds. Some of these seeds will grow into new maple trees.

The life cycle of cone bearing, or **coniferous**, trees, such as pine trees, begins with seeds that grow inside cones. Wing-shaped seeds fall out of the cones. Wind helps them "fly" like helicopters to new places where they can grow.

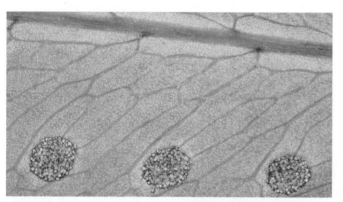

■ **Non-flowering plants, such as ferns, grow from spores, not seeds.**

■ **Bristlecone pine trees are some of the oldest living things on Earth. Some have lived for more than 4,000 years.**

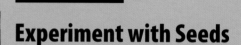

Activity

Experiment with Seeds

Experiment with fast-growing seeds, such as radish seeds or grass seeds. These grow well inside your house and outside.

1. Draw a picture of the seeds you use.
2. Experiment with different ways to grow the seeds. Here are some ideas.
   • Grow your seeds in different kinds of soil.
   • Grow them with different amounts of water.
   • Grow them in different temperatures.
   • Grow them in different amounts of light.
3. Draw more pictures to show how your seeds change and grow.
4. When your experiments are finished, draw pictures showing the life cycles of the plants you grew.

Seeds, Cones, and Flowers

Plants that grow from seeds have something in common with animals. Like animals, seed plants need **eggs** and **sperm** to reproduce. Seed plants have male parts for producing sperm and female parts for producing eggs.

Seeds from Coniferous Trees

Coniferous trees, such as spruce, have male cones and female cones. The male cones produce grains of **pollen** that contain sperm. The female cones produce eggs. Each spring, male cones release millions of pollen grains. Seeds form if the sperm inside a pollen grain joins with the egg inside a female cone.

■ **Female cones are hard and large, while male cones are soft and small.**

Seeds from Flowering Plants

People often refer to flowers as plants. Flowers are not plants; they are parts of plants. An amazing variety of flowers exists in our world. They come in all shapes, sizes, and colors. Whether they are large or small, yellow or purple, spiky or umbrella-shaped, all flowers have the same important role to play. Their role is to form seeds so that new flowering plants can grow.

The male parts of flowers are the **stamens**, which contain sperm. The female part is the **pistil**, which produces eggs. The pistil is sticky on top so that it can catch pollen that falls on it. The movement of pollen from the stamens to the pistil is called **pollination**.

Activity

Do Some Research

Some plants pollinate themselves. The pollen moves from the stamens to the pistil of the same plant. Many plants have to be cross-pollinated. This means that the pollen has to come from a different plant of the same kind. Find out how bees, hummingbirds, butterflies, and moths help plants cross-pollinate.

Traveling Seeds

Seeds need certain growing conditions to sprout and develop. What do you think would happen if seeds always fell on the ground beside or under their parent plant? They would have to compete for the same light, water, and minerals as their parent. Often, they would not survive. Seeds have ways to move and find new places to grow.

■ **Light, fluffy dandelion seeds are carried by the wind.**

Puzzler

Have you ever helped seeds travel to a place where they can sprout and grow?

Answer: You probably have. Maybe some burrs got stuck on your socks or pants when you visited a park or a ravine. Maybe you spit out some watermelon or orange seeds when you were on a picnic.

■ Tumbleweed seeds are scattered when the wind blows the whole plant around.

■ Hound's-tongue seeds hitchhike. Sharp spikes surround the seeds. When an animal brushes past, the spikes get tangled in its fur.

15

Fabulous Fruit

What is your favorite fruit? Is it a sweet, juicy watermelon, a tangy orange, or a crunchy almond? Scientists think of almonds and other nuts as fruit.

■ **Watermelons are heavy because they are 92 percent water.**

All flowering plants have fruit. Some fruits are soft and fleshy, and others are hard and dry. Some are so large that you can barely lift them. Others are so tiny that you can barely see them. Fruits are the parts of flowering plants that contain and protect the seeds.

■ Strawberries are soft fruits because they do not have pits.

Activity

Grouping Fruit

This photograph shows a number of fruits. Group them into different categories, such as size, shape, and color. Show this book to some friends, and ask them to make their own groups. Do you agree with them? Do they agree with you?

Habitat

Plants live almost anywhere you can imagine. The places where plants live and grow are called their **habitats**. Different habitats on Earth receive different amounts of rain and sunshine, and experience different kinds of temperatures.

Conditions

Tropical Forests	Northern Forests	Temperate Forests
hot temperatures and plenty of rainfall	fairly long, cold winters and fairly short, mild summers	cold winters and warm, wet summers

Examples climbing vines, evergreen trees, ferns, large-leafed trees, orchids	**Examples** coniferous evergreen trees, mosses, wildflowers	**Examples** **deciduous** trees, geraniums, tiger lilies

These three things—rain, sunlight, and temperature—affect the kinds of plants that can grow in the various habitats. Some plants, such as Arctic poppies, have **adapted** to cold, dry habitats. Their seeds survive the long, harsh Arctic winter and blossom in the spring. Other plants, such as orchids, have adapted to hot, wet habitats. They grow in humid tropical rain forests and can live in very wet areas.

Grasslands	Deserts	Arctic
dry, cold winters and warm, damp summers	very hot and dry all year long	very long, cold, dry winters and very short, warm summers
Examples clover, grasses, poppies	**Examples** cactus plants, desert lilies, yucca plants	**Examples** Arctic poppies, Arctic willow trees, mosses

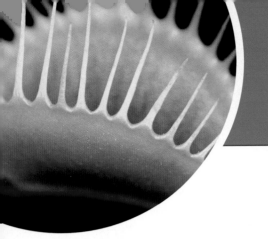

Have You Met a Tree Surgeon?

Trees and other plants can get sick, just as people and animals can. A tree surgeon is a person who takes care of trees when their roots, stems, leaves, or branches are diseased. Sometimes, a tree surgeon will carefully trim diseased branches from trees. Other times, the tree may have holes in it that need filling. Fruit farmers sometimes call in tree surgeons to look after their fruit and nut trees or their grapevines. Most tree surgeons are self-employed. This means that they run their own business, and people hire them for small or big jobs. Would you like to be a tree surgeon?

■ Trees sometimes need to be trimmed to stay healthy.

Activity

Do Your Own Research

Ask a parent or teacher to help you discover if you are interested in these plant careers:

- botanist
- carpenter
- farmer
- forestry worker

- greenhouse grower
- parks and recreation worker
- soil scientist

Strange Plants

Animals are not the only meat-eaters on Earth. Some plants eat meat, too! These plants usually live in damp, swampy places where nutrients are in short supply. The insects they eat help them stay healthy.

■ The leaves of the Venus flytrap spring shut when an insect lands on the trigger hairs.

■ The pitcher plant collects rainwater to drown its insect prey.

Puzzler

Are there any foods you eat that do not come from plants in some way?

Answer: Salt does not come from plants. It is a mineral. Other than salt, plants probably play a role in everything you eat.

21

Food and Flavoring

Do you like cookies and milk? What about green salads and fruit salads? Maybe you put ketchup on hamburgers. Do you shake pepper on your eggs?

■ **Doughnuts are deep-fried in oil. Oil is made from plants such as corn, canola, and peanuts.**

All these foods depend on plants. Cookies are made with flour. Flour comes from a type of plant called wheat. Cows produce milk. They are fed plants such as hay, oats, and barley.

Vegetables and fruits are plants. Ketchup is made from tomatoes that grow on tomato plants. Pepper is a spice. It is ground from the small, dried berries of a pepper plant.

■ Spices and herbs come from different parts of plants. They are used to give food more flavor.

23

Chemicals from Plants

Plants contain chemicals that are used to make all kinds of helpful products. This is especially true of the chemicals that are used to make medicine. The bark of the willow tree contains a chemical that helps when you have a fever or a headache. You may have heard of the medicine we make from this chemical. It is called aspirin.

■ Paints are made from plant chemicals.

Even though we use plant chemicals every day, many of them are poisonous. When they are used incorrectly or carelessly, they can make people and animals sick. In some cases, they can cause death. You should never touch plants that you do not recognize.

■ Tea plants grow on large plantations.

Puzzler

Have you ever heard of poison ivy? Do you know what it does?

Answer: Poison ivy contains a chemical that causes skin to become red, swollen, and itchy. Some people and animals have severe reactions to poison ivy that require medical treatment. Usually, though, the itchiness and swelling go away after several days.

Plant Fibers

All plants contain hairlike strands called fibers. Life would be very different without the products that are made from these valuable plant materials.

Fibers for Building

You live in plants all the time. Most of the houses and buildings you see around you are made from wood. Wooden building materials are made of fibers that come mainly from the trunks of trees. The center part of the tree is used to make long beams and wide boards. That is because the fibers in the center are very strong and firm. Fibers from the outer parts of the tree are used for making flexible boards, such as plywood.

What other animals use plant fibers in their everyday lives?

Answer: A fish called the stickleback builds a nest with twigs and sticks. Birds build their nests from the leaves and stems of different plants. Squirrels use the same materials for their nests, too. Birds and squirrels also build their nests with paper that has ended up in nature.

Fibers for Paper

You write on plants all the time. Most paper is made with fibers that come from the stems of trees. Other plant fibers are used to make paper products, too. In some countries, such as Canada, paper money is made with flax fibers.

Fibers for Clothing

You wear plants every day. Many of the fabrics used to make clothing come from plant fibers. Cotton fiber comes from the seeds of cotton plants. Linen fiber comes from the stems of flax plants. Plant fibers are also used to make ropes, bed sheets, and chair coverings.

27

Plants in Danger

Earth's human population grows larger every minute of every day. We all need food to eat, building materials to make houses, and fibers to make fabrics and clothing.

Most importantly, we need space to live. However, to make this space, we have to clear away the very living things that provide us with all the other things we need—plants.

Over the past 100 years, humans have endangered the lives of many kinds of plants. Right now, more than one out of every ten kinds of plants on Earth is in danger of becoming **extinct**. Some countries have laws to save special areas for plants.

■ **Some yew trees live for hundreds of years.**

■ Sometimes, seedlings are planted in forests that have been cut down.

■ Trees in rain forests are often cut down to build roads and farmland.

How can you help plants?

1. Do you recycle paper instead of putting it in the garbage? Do you use recycled paper and products made from recycled paper, such as toilet paper and paper towels? Recycling paper means we need to destroy fewer trees for their fiber.

2. When you are outside, do you watch where you walk? Be careful. Plants are everywhere around you. Remember the plants the next time you play in a park or hike in a nature area.

3. What happens to the food you do not finish? Do you throw it away? Fruits, vegetables, and other plant parts can be composted and mixed with soil to enrich it and grow new plants.

Design Your Own Garden

Plants are necessary to the survival of living things. They are also beautiful, and many of them smell wonderful. Plants are a welcome sight outside and inside.

Why not grow some plants for yourself? Ask a family member or a friend to help. Maybe you could get some advice from neighbors who like to grow their own plants or have a garden.

■ **Herbs can be grown in a garden, flower pot, or window box.**

Some people grow their own vegetables instead of buying them at a grocery store.

Growing a Garden

1. Start by deciding what kind of garden you would like to grow.

 • Would you like to grow plants so you can admire their colors?

 • Would you like to grow plants so you can admire their smells?

 • Would you like to grow vegetables or herbs so you can flavor and enjoy food that you have grown yourself?

2. Next, decide where you will grow your plants, and find out what supplies you will need.

 • Will you grow them outside or inside?

 • What kind of soil will you need?

 • Will you grow them from seeds, or will you start with young plants that have already sprouted?

 • How often will you need to water them?

 • How much sunshine will they need?

Glossary

adapted: became suited to a certain environment or way of life by changing gradually over a long period of time

carbon dioxide: a colorless, odorless gas that plants use to make food

chlorophyll: a green-colored substance that plants use to make food from water, carbon dioxide, and sunlight

coniferous: trees that bear cones

deciduous: a tree or shrub that sheds its leaves each year

eggs: female reproductive cells

extinct: no longer in existence

habitats: the places where living things live and grow

oxygen: a colorless, odorless gas that is found in water and air

pistil: the female part of a plant; it produces eggs

pollen: grains that contain sperm that is used in reproduction

pollination: the transfer of pollen from the male part of a plant to the female part of a plant

reproduce: to join together to create new living things

sperm: male reproductive cells

stamens: the male parts of plants; they produce pollen

Index

Websites

www.urbanext.uiuc.edu/gpe
http://plants.usda.gov

www.kidsgardening.com
http://rainforestheroes.com

Some websites stay current longer than others. For further websites, use your search engines to locate topics such as flowers, gardens, plants, and trees.